ONE MILLION STRONG

A PHOTOGRAPHIC TRIBUTE
OF THE
MILLION MAN MARCH

AFFIRMATIONS FOR THE AFRICAN-AMERICAN MALE

PHOTOGRAPHS BY
RODERICK TERRY

COVER DESIGN, PAGE LAYOUT AND TEXT COMPOSITION BY
CLIFF GILES OF CLIFF ART GRAPHICS STUDIO

Duncan & Duncan, Inc.
Publishers

"*I would be nothing else in God's creation but a Black Man.*"

– Marcus Garvey

ONE MILLION STRONG–
A Photographic Tribute of the Million Man March
© July 1996 by Roderick Terry

Published by:
Duncan & Duncan, Inc., Publishers
Address correspondence and orders to:
2809 Pulaski Highway
P.O. Box 1137
Edgewood, MD 21040
Telephone: 410-538-5579: Fax: 410-538-5584

We gratefully acknowledge permission to reprint the following photographs
by Frank Franklin: "Men at the Mall," page 20; "Rosa Parks," page 63; "Minister Farrakhan," page 89

Library of Congress Catalog Card Data: 96-85705

Additional CIP Data:
Terry, Roderick
ONE MILLION STRONG
1. Afro-American men 2. Afro-American men, photographic tribute 3. Affirmations and inspiration for the Afro-American
man 4. Afro-American culture 5. Afro-American history 6. Million Man March

Cover design, page layout and composition design by Cliff Giles of Cliff Art Graphics Studio, located in Abingdon, Maryland.

ISBN: 1-878647-29-6

10 9 8 7 6 5 4 3 2 1

"*I call on you my sons to straighten out your backs and stand on your feet with a strong determination to proclaim your rightful place in this world in righteousness and in divine order.*"

– Queen Mother Moore

DEDICATION

For my brother Fred Terry, III, and all of the brothers in the struggle.

ACKNOWLEDGMENT

I would like to express my heartfelt gratitude to the following individuals for their support and encouragement during the completion of this book:

Nancy Lyons, Juanita Dean, Vickey Wright, Tracey Moore, Jocelyn Winston, Carla Robinson and Dr. Ray Howell.

INTRODUCTION

The Million Man March on Washington was a defining moment in the history of African-American men. On October 16, 1995, in a demonstration of solidarity, pride and unity, more than one million black men crowded the length and width of the National Mall, between the U.S. Capitol and the Washington Monument, transforming it into a beautiful "sea of blackness." This day of atonement and reconciliation brought together black men from virtually every state and territory in America.

The March was a clarion call for black men to take control of their destinies. It ignited a movement among African-American men toward self-realization, character building and empowerment, bringing new ideas, strategies and solutions to the problems that beset black communities. William E.B. DuBois' statement, "There is within this world no such force as the force of a man determined to rise," resounds today with truth and urgency.

The time is ripe for African-American men to rise above cultural stereotypes and social and economic deprivation, and through brotherhood, build a new nation based on equal justice, personal responsibility, hard work and a devotion to God.

ONE MILLION STRONG is a photographic tribute to the courageous men who participated in the Million Man March. During the March, I observed and captured with my camera faces replete with human emotions. Creased lines in their foreheads revealed the seriousness of purpose and intensity of the marchers. Glistening, broad smiling faces personified the jubilation, joy, and pride of men who had come together for the first time in history to bond on common ground. I could literally feel the human warmth and camaraderie exploding around me.

Their eyes were the most telling. In spite of the air of love, peacefulness and the calmness that engulfed the mall, a look into their eyes revealed the deep pain, long suffering and racial injustices that precipitated the Million Man March. I felt my brothers outcry for atonement, equal justice, and fair play. Poet, Maya Angelou, in her eloquent manner summed up our frustrations with, "The night has been long, the pit has been dark, the wall has been steep."

The feelings generated by the abundance of positive messages heard were so strong and overwhelming that the intrusiveness of my camera was seldom noticed which allowed me to capture spontaneous, unposed, and surprising moments revealing true feelings and emotions.

I have attempted to show, through these photographs, the hope, emotion, and struggle that defines the African-American male's experience and the black man's desire to unite and uplift the black race. *ONE MILLION STRONG* also contains words of wisdom and motivational thoughts which are intended to motivate, inspire and nurture the actions of black men everywhere.

I sincerely hope the courage of these "million" men, who came to Washington to protest the status quo and demand that their voices be heard, inspires you.

Roderick Terry

"*The Establishment will escalate blacks up to the mezzanine floor or higher. It will elevate them to the topmost floors, and it will airlift them to the plane's cruising altitude, but it will not lift them one basis point up the ladder of power. The heftiness for that hoist must come from blacks themselves.*"

– T.M. Pryor

"*There are rare instances when truth is best served by silence.*"

– Gordon Parks

"*You were not expected to aspire to excellence; you were expected to make peace with mediocrity.*"

– James Baldwin

"*If you live in an oppressive society, you've got to be resilent. You can't let each little thing crush you. You have to take every encounter and make yourself larger, rather than allow yourself to be diminished by it.*"

– James Earl Jones

"Our sense of self as black people is always under attack in this society, but it's reaffirmed and enhanced at the moment you take a stance."

– Derrick Bell

"*I decided that purpose, meaning, and order in nature emanated from God and that the same must be true for me.*"

– Andrew Young

"They can laugh, but they can't deny us. They can curse and kill us, but they can't destroy us. This land is ours because we come out of it, we bled in it, our tears watered it, we fertilized it with our dead. So the more of us they destroy, the more it becomes filled with the spirit of our redemption."

– Ralph Ellison

"*You should concentrate on the heights which you are determined to reach, not look back into the depths to which you once fell.*"

– Dr. Martin Luther King, Jr.

"*You watch your back. You don't take things for granted. You work real hard and you fight for what you believe in.*"

– Kweisi Mfume

"*Look at the faces here. Where is the nigger?
And if he is not here, where is he?
And if he never was, why was he?*"

– Anonymous

"*America's greatest crime against the black man was not slavery or lynching, but that he was taught to wear a mask of self-hate and self-doubt.*"

– Malcolm X

"If a man is called to be a street sweeper, he should sweep streets even as Michelangelo painted, or as Beethoven composed music, or as Shakespeare wrote poetry. He should sweep streets so well that all the hosts of heaven and earth will pause to say, here lived a great street sweeper who did his job well."

– Dr. Martin Luther King, Jr.

"*We realize that our future lies chiefly in our own hands. We know that neither institution nor friends can make a race stand unless it has strength in its own foundation. In order to succeed it must practice the virtues of self-reliance, self-respect, industry, perseverance and economy.*"

– Paul Robeson

" *Start where you are with what you have, knowing that what you have is plenty enough.*"

– Booker T. Washington

"*Each of us must earn our own existence. And how does anyone earn anything?
Through perserverance, hard work, and desire.*"

– Thurgood Marshall

"*Do what is required of you and remain a slave.*
Do more than is required and become free."

– Marcus Garvey

"*He who starts behind in the race of life must forever remain behind or run faster than the man in front.*"

— Dr. Benjamin E. Mays

"As long as hope remains and meaning is preserved, the possibility of overcoming oppression stays alive."

– Dr. Cornel West

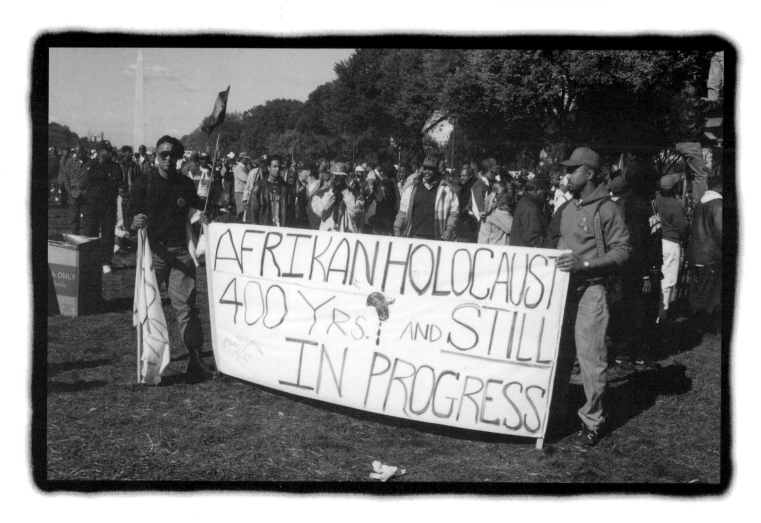

"*I learned in moments of humiliation to walk away with what was left of my dignity, rather than lose it all in an explosion of rage. I learned to raise my eyes to the high moral ground, and to stake my future on it.*"

– Arthur Ashe

"There is something in every one of you that waits
and listens for the sound of genuine in yourself.
It is the only true guide you will ever have.
And if you cannot hear it, you will all of your
life spend your days on the ends of string
that somebody else pulls."

– Howard Thurman

"*When I discover who I am,
I'll be free.*"

– Ralph Ellison

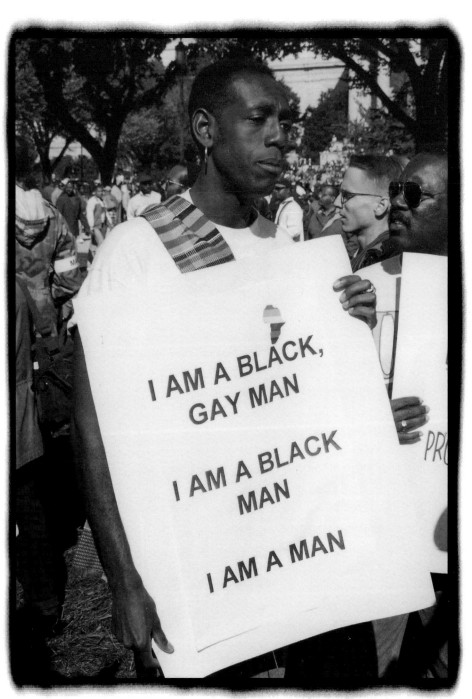

"*I have observed that those who have accomplished the greatest results are those who "keep under the body"; are those who never grow excited or lose self-control, but are always calm, self-possessed, patient, and polite.*"

– Booker T. Washington

" *True peace is not merely the absence of tension
but the presence of justice and brotherhood.*"

– Dr. Martin Luther King, Jr.

"*The sky is the limit. Let us continue to dream. Dreaming is a gift of the spirit that can lift you above the misery to miracles and allow you to smile through tears.*"

– Rev. Jesse Jackson

"*I* *would crawl on my hands and knees through mud and mire, to the feet of a learned man, where I would sit and humbly supplicate him to instill into me that which neither devils nor tyrants could remove. For colored people to acquire learning in this country make tyrants quake and tremble on their sandy foundations.*"

– David Walker

"*Out of the heart are the issues of life and no external force, however great and overwhelming, can at long last destroy a people if it does not first win the victory of the spirit against them.*"

– Howard Thurman

"*I would rather go to hell by choice than stumble into heaven by following the crowd.*"

– Dr. Benjamin E. Mays

"This new day gives us yet another chance, my friends, to turn dreams into realities, to turn impossibilities into possibilities and lift spirits to begin to believe, to begin to hope, to turn fear into faith and look forward and not backward."

– Marion Barry

"Nothing in the world is more dangerous
than a sincere ignorance
and conscientious stupidity."

– Dr. Martin Luther King, Jr.

"*Power recognizes only power, and all of them who realize this have made gains.*"

– Malcolm X

"Know from whence you come. If you know whence you came, there is really no limit to where you can go."

– James Baldwin

"*One thing they cannot prohibit–*
The strong men...comin' on
The strong men gittin' stronger.
Stronger..."

– Sterling Brown

"Life is ultimately a challenge and a discipline."

– Dr. Cornel West

BUSINESS AND OUR TOMORROW

I want to share with you some points of view which I think you and I must inevitably come to grips with and adopt as accepted policy and procedure if we are to be a part of the mainstream of the American economy. I want to preface my remarks with a description of the three classes of people we have to encounter in any attempt to move from mediocrity or the status-quo to new plateaus of economic, political, or social responsibility.

Throughout history, change has been accompanied by disturbance and unrest. Men and nations either rise to greater heights of valor and character or sink to unprecedented depths of brutality and cowardice. In such a time, there is a sharp shifting of the goat and the sheep—no individual, race, or nation can escape the process. In such a time, there also emerges three groups with at least three points of view relative to the course to be followed. They emerged in the wilderness with Moses and they are no less imminent today.

First, there are those who resent change and the adjustments and the discipline which new concepts impose. They cling blindly to the past and, like the children of Israel, would rather go back to the fleshpots of Pharaoh and enslave their children's children than sacrifice and earn the freedom and abundance of a Promised Land.

The second group aren't quite willing to return to the enslavement of yesteryears, but neither are they adventurous enough to move forward to the freedom of tomorrow. They are the, "let-well-enough-do-crowd or "let's just be satisfied with what we've got and where we are." They are willing to stand by and let whosoever will go forward, clear the way, solve the problems, make the rough places smooth and the crooked straight. With this assurance, once it's safe and the objective has been secured, they will organize a great phalanxes and move in one great mass and help enjoy the spoils of victory.

The last group, I call the Creative Minority, and since the beginning of time, they have always been in the minority. These are the ones who have accomplished everything. They have accomplished the welfare of the world, and passed onto unborn generations a legacy of respectability, hope, and courage, that has lifted them from the malarious damps of the lowlands, out of inertia and inarticulate concern, into the sunlight of boundless horizons. It is this Creative Minority to which you and I must belong.

T.M. Alexander, Sr.

Reprinted with permission from
Beyond the Timberline: The Trials and Triumphs of a Black Entrepreneur
© 1992 Duncan & Duncan, Inc.

"We know that we are beautiful."

— Langston Hughes

"*We'd better pull together before the forces pull us apart.*"

– Willie Brown

"*If a man hasn't discovered
something that he will die for,
he isn't fit to live.*"

– Dr. Martin Luther King, Jr.

"*If you can control a man's thinking, you do not have to worry about his action. When you determine what a man shall think you do not have to concern yourself about what he will do. If you make a man feel that he is inferior, you do not have to compel him to accept an inferior status, for he will seek it himself. If you make a man think that he is justly outcast, you do not have to order him to the back door. He will go without being told; and if there is no back door, his very nature will demand one.*"

– Carter G. Woodson

"Don't give up; don't give out; and don't give in!"

– Arthur A. Fletcher

"No man is really free who is afraid to speak the truth as he knows it is, or who is too fearful to take a stand for that which he knows is right."

– Dr. Benjamin E. Mays

"*If there is no struggle, there is no progress. Those who profess to favor freedom, and yet deprecate agitation, are people who want crops without plowing up the ground.*"

– Frederick Douglass

"*God created us so that we should form the human family, existing together because we were made for one another. We are not made for an exclusive self-sufficiency but for interdependence, and we break the law of being at our peril.*"

– Desmond Tutu

"It is within our power to dream, to build air castles, to think great thoughts, to aim at the stars and grasp the moon."

– Dr. Benjamin E. Mays

"*Question everything. Every stripe,
every star, every word spoken.
Question everything.*"

– Ernest Gaines

"To love life is to be whole in all one's parts;
and to be whole in all one's parts
is to be free and unafraid."

– Howard Thurman

"*Every person of humane convictions must decide on the protest that best suits his convictions, but we must all protest.*"

– Dr. Martin Luther King, Jr.

"We must use time creatively, and forever realize
that the time is always ripe to do right."

– Nelson Mandela

"Thicken the thunders of man's voice, and lo! a world awakes."

– W.E.B. DuBois

"We ourselves have the power to end the terror and win for ourselves peace and security. We have the power of numbers, the power of organization, and the power of spirit."

– Paul Robeson

"*Where there is hope there is life, where there is life there is possibility and where there is possibility change can occur.*"

– Rev. Jesse Jackson, Jr.

"*For while the tale of how we suffer, and how we are delighted, and how we may triumph is never new, it always must be heard. There isn't any other tale to tell, it's the only light we've got in all this darkness.*"

– James Baldwin

"*As an African-American woman, I am proud, applaud and support our men in this assemblage.*"

– Rosa Parks

"*Before the ship of your life reaches its last harbor, there will be long drawn-out storms, howling and jostling winds, and tempestuous seas that make the heart stand still. If you do not have a deep and patient faith in God, you will be powerless to face the delay, disappointment, and vicissitudes that inevitably come.*"

– Dr. Martin Luther King, Jr.

"Let us not waste time in breathless appeals to the strong while we are weak, but lend our time, energy, and effort to the accumulation of strength among ourselves by which we will voluntarily

attract the attention of others."

– Marcus Garvey

"*A wise man who has the moment in his hand should not let the moment slip.*"

– Nelson Mandela

"*You are not judged by the height you have risen, but from the depths you climbed.*"

– Marcus Garvey

"*He who is not courageous enough to take risks will accomplish nothing in life.*"

– Muhammad Ali

"*Experience has taught me that man is never quite so near to success as when that which he calls failure has nearly overtaken him.*"

– Dennis Kimbro

"*Mix a conviction with a man
and something happens.*"

– Adam Clayton Powell, Jr.

"We cannot afford to settle for being just average; we must learn as much as we can to be the best that we can. The key is education–that's knowledge–
education with maximum effort."

– Bill Cosby

"*If I were you, I would stand for something; I would count for something and no man would push me around because my skin is black or his eyes are blue. I would stand for something. I would count.*"

– Benjamin E. Mays

"*All human beings are periodically tested by the power of the universe…and how one performs under pressure is the true measure of one's spirit, heart, and desire.*"

– Spike Lee

"*Find the good. It's all around you.
Find it, showcase it
and you'll start believing in it.*"

– Jesse Owens

"*Judge not thy brother. There are secrets in his heart that you might weep to see.*"

– Egbert Martin

"*One can only face in others*
what one can face in oneself."

– James Baldwin

"*Be, in reality, all that you appear to be. Don't give the impression of being anything but yourself. That is precisely what you have got to deal with, live with, and manage for better or worse, the rest of your life.*"

– T.M. Alexander, Sr.

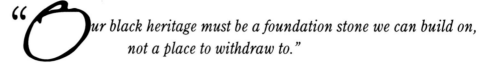

"Our black heritage must be a foundation stone we can build on, not a place to withdraw to."

– Colin L. Powell

"*One of the ways by which men measure their significance is to be found in the amount of power and energy other men use in order to crunch them or hold them back…The persecution becomes a vote of confidence, which becomes, in turn, a source of inspiration, power and validation.*"

– Howard Thurman

"*I find, in being black, a thing of beauty—a joy, a strength, a secret cup of gladness...*"

– Ossie Davis

"*It must be borne in mind that the tragedy of life does not lie in not reaching your goals, the tragedy lies in not having any goals to reach. It isn't a calamity to die with dreams unfulfilled, but it is a calamity not to dream. It is not a disaster to be unable to capture your ideals, but it is a disaster to have no ideals to capture. It is not a disgrace not to reach the stars, but it is a disgrace to have no stars to reach.*"

– Dr. Benjamin E. Mays

"*Blacks will have to be equally as determined and committed to public policy on black self-empowerment as white society has been to public policy on the use of blacks.*"

– Dr. Claud Anderson

"*It is not your environment, it is you - the quality of your mind, the integrity of your soul and the determination of your will that will decide your future and shape your lives.*"

– Dr. Benjamin E. Mays

"My contemplation of life…taught me that he who cannot change the very fabric of his thought…will never be able to change reality, and will never, therefore, make any progress."

– Anwar Sadat

"The only way to solve a problem that is unjust is
to take immediate action to correct it."

– Malcolm X

"*We create our own destiny by the way we do things. We have to take advantage of opportunities and be responsible for our choices.*"

– Dr. Benjamin Carson

"*I beg of you to remember that whenever our life touches yours, we help or hinder…whenever your life touches ours, you make us stronger or weaker…There is no escape - man drags man down, or man lifts man up.*"

– Booker T. Washington

The Million Man March Pledge

I — pledge that from this day forward, I will strive to love my brother as I love myself.

I — from this day forward, will strive to improve myself spiritually, morally, mentally, socially, politically and economically for the benefit of myself, my family and my people.

I — pledge that I will strive to build business, build houses, build hospitals, build factories and enter into international trade for the good of myself, my family and my people.

I — pledge that from this day forward, I will never raise my hand with a knife or a gun to beat, cut or shoot any member of my family or any human being except in self defense.

I — pledge from this day forward, I will never abuse my wife by striking her, disrespecting her, for she is the mother of my children and the producer of my future.

I — pledge that from this day forward, I will never engage in the abuse of children, little boys or little girls, for sexual gratification. But I will let them grow in peace to be strong men and women for the future of our people.

I — will never again use the "b" word to describe any female, but particularly my own Black sister.

I — pledge that from this day forward, that I will not poison my body with drugs or that which is destructive to my health and my well-being.

I — pledge from this day forward, that I will support Black newspapers, Black radio, Black television. I will support Black artists who clean up their acts and show respect for themselves and respect for their people and respect for the heirs of the human family.

I — will do all of this, so help me God.

– Minister Louis Farrakhan

ONE
MILLION
STRONG